Cash Carriers

Andrew Buxton

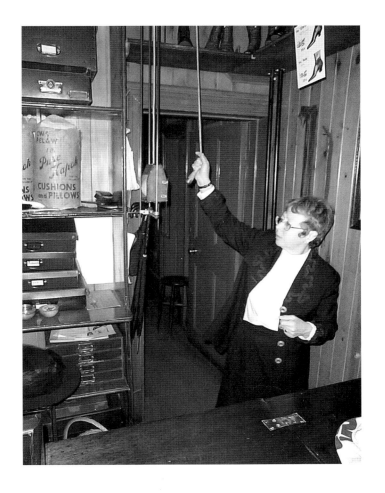

A Shire book

CONTENTS

Cover: *The Lamson Cash System in the Co-op Hardware Department at Beamish, the North of England Open Air Museum, County Durham, being worked by Tom Stevens.*

Title page: *Another view of the Beamish system: the ball is raised in the lift by Dorothy Carlyon, the senior demonstrator. See also page 6.*

ACKNOWLEDGEMENTS

I am greatly indebted to John Liffen of the Science Museum, London, who supplied much information and suggested several improvements. I also thank the many shop staff, museum staff and collectors who gave me information and helped with photographs, particularly the North of England Open Air Museum at Beamish, Jacksons of Reading, the Cumberland Toy and Model Museum, Arding & Hobbs of Clapham Junction and Bromsgrove Museum.

Illustrations are acknowledged as follows: Beamish, the North of England Open Air Museum, County Durham, front cover; by permission of the British Library, pages 21, 23; Byron Collection, Museum of the City of New York, page 11; Mr Alex Joyce, page 20 (bottom); Kentish Times Newspapers, page 16 (top); Lamson Engineering Company Ltd, page 8; Leicester City Museums Service, page 3; Mr Eric Meadows, pages 14, 15 (all); Ms Joan Miller, page 12 (both); Mr Rod Moore, Cumberland Toy and Model Museum, page 22 (all); *This England*, page 9 (both).

British Library Cataloguing in Publication Data: Buxton, Andrew. Cash carriers in shops. – (Shire album; 438) 1. Retail trade – Equipment and supplies. 2. Retail trade – Equipment and supplies – Pictorial works I. Title. 381.1'0284. ISBN 0 7478 0615 2.

Published in 2004 by Shire Publications Ltd, Cromwell House, Church Street, Princes Risborough, Buckinghamshire HP27 9AA, UK. (Website: www.shirebooks.co.uk)
Copyright © 2004 by Andrew Buxton. First published 2004. Shire Album 438. ISBN 0 7478 0615 2.
Andrew Buxton is hereby identified as the author of this work in accordance with Section 77 of the Copyright, Designs and Patents Act 1988.

Printed in Great Britain by CIT Printing Services Ltd, Press Buildings, Merlins Bridge, Haverfordwest, Pembrokeshire SA61 1XF.

HOW AND WHY CASH CARRIERS WERE USED

The business of a shop is to exchange goods for money. In the shops of the nineteenth century it was usual to have a single cashier or cash office to receive all payments and to issue change (or, for wealthier customers, to record details on their accounts). This system was later known as cash centralisation. It meant that only one trustworthy cashier was needed to handle the cash and record transactions and the temptation for the sales assistants to pilfer was removed. Either the assistant would go to the office or the customers would go themselves. In the United States of America cash boys or cash girls were sometimes employed to carry the payments and change. The assistant would call out 'Cash' and the child would rush to carry the money. Some contemporary accounts draw attention to the long hours and poor conditions in which these children worked.

In the mid 1870s inventors began to think about how this operation might be automated. It is said that in William Lamson's shop at Lowell, Massachusetts, the sales staff used to tie the cash up in a handkerchief and throw it across to the cashier. Another version is that the money was wrapped up in the receipt. Lamson then came up with the idea of using a wooden ball, like a hollowed-out croquet ball, which could be taken apart into two halves. The money was placed inside and held by a spring; the ball was reassembled and then put on a track that sloped down to the cashier. The cashier dealt with the transaction and returned the receipt and any change along another track that sloped in the other direction,

The cash-ball system from the Beehive haberdasher's shop in Silver Street, Leicester. It was reconstructed at the Leicester Museum of Costume, which is now closed. In this reconstruction the two tracks have been installed parallel, whereas they should be sloping in opposite directions.

down to the 'station' at the sales point. Other shops wanted similar systems and Lamson founded a company in Boston that within a few years spread around the world.

There were many advantages. Because the change was counted out in the cash office and again by the sales assistant, error and fraud were virtually eliminated. The customer remained with the assistant at the counter and so might be encouraged to make further purchases. Congestion due to staff or customers moving about was minimised. Cash floats were not required at every sales point. Cash carriers were also used to carry dockets to the office so that purchases on account could be authorised.

The cash-ball system was quite intrusive and expensive to install. It required a large amount of space at the cash desk. Cable systems, where the carriers were fixed to a moving cable, succeeded the cash-ball system in the USA but do not seem to have been used much in Britain. The best-known system in Britain is the Rapid Wire, where the carrier was suspended from a fixed wire by two pulleys. It was propelled by a catapult-like device, operated by pulling a cord. Barr's system, subsequently developed by Gipe, used two wires that were pulled apart to propel the carriage.

Pneumatic tube systems had been in use for carrying messages and documents from about the 1850s. In 1880 John Wanamaker introduced them in his store for carrying cash. In larger stores, where the cash office might be quite a distance from the sales points and serve several floors, pneumatic tube systems were more suitable than cash balls or wire systems. The cash office could be sited in an area that was not prime selling space, such as the top floor or the basement (although one of the reasons for later abandoning cash centralisation was that staff did not like working in such areas).

A common objection to centralised systems was the time taken to give change to the customer. In the largest buildings with pneumatic tubes the time from the farthest station to the tube room might be up to twenty seconds. Cashiers could handle about four to six transactions per minute, so the total time might be up to a minute. However, at busy times the cashiers might get overloaded and customers would get impatient, especially because they could not see that their transaction was being dealt with.

The downfall of the cash carrier came with the widespread use of cash registers and then the rise of the self-service store. The principal inventor of the cash register was James Ritty for his saloon in Dayton, Ohio, in 1879. It allowed security of cash handling at each sales point rather than at a central office. Cash registers were often introduced first into the quick-selling, small goods departments (probably on the ground floor), with a centralised system being retained elsewhere. Arnotts of Dublin was one of the stores to change over in this way. Before cash registers were installed in busy departments its pneumatic tube system was unable to cope at lunchtime and the senior superintendent resorted to giving change out of his own pocket. Also at sales times many items sold for one penny, but sales dockets still had to be written in duplicate for each transaction. They got scribbled illegibly, and careless customers covered the floor with their copies. Some of the larger stores, after going over to cash registers, retained carriers as a relief measure in busy departments at peak periods of trade, such as the Christmas season. Self-service stores started in the USA in 1916 and took off in Britain with Co-ops in the 1940s.

Now only a few cash carriers remain in service, mainly as curiosities, and there are several in museums. The main problem in later years was obtaining spares, and shops resorted to substituting clothes lines for the cords, having parts made specially for them, or doing repairs themselves. Pneumatic tubes are still in use for other purposes, however, and for carrying cash in bulk from checkouts to secure storage in supermarkets, rather than letting it build up near the exit or having to carry it through the store.

LAMSON AND THE CASH-BALL SYSTEM

W. S. Lamson and the Lamson Company

William Stickney Lamson was born in Newburyport, Massachusetts, in 1845. After working as a commercial artist and a soldier, he opened a shop in Merrimack Street, Lowell, in February 1879, where he installed his cash-carrying system. On 3rd December 1879 he filed a patent for a system with inclined rails fixed to the walls of the shop. There were, however, earlier patents for systems to carry money in stores. In 1875 David Brown of New Jersey had patented a system with a carriage running on a wire rail and propelled by an endless rope.

In 1882 the Lamson Cash Carrier Company was incorporated in Boston, Massachusetts. Business expanded quickly and by 1885 there were installations in nearly six hundred stores in the USA. As the company grew and absorbed rivals there were several changes in name. By 1888 it was called the Lamson Consolidated Store Service Company, which in 1912 was simplified to the Lamson Company.

John Magrath Kelly became the British agent for the cash-ball system in 1885. The following year the agency was operating from premises at 1 Charlotte Street, London W1. The cellar was a storeroom, the ground floor the factory and the first-floor accommodation for Kelly and his family. Some early sales must be reflected in the advertisement in *The Times* of 29th December 1887 by a cashier 'thoroughly conversant with the Lamson Store Service system' seeking an engagement. Business flourished and on 9th August 1888 the Lamson Store Service Company Ltd was incorporated. The new company had rights to the ball system for the 'eastern hemisphere', in other words Europe, Africa, Australia, New Zealand and the Middle East. An agent was appointed in Sydney, Australia, in 1889. In 1892 the factory was moved to Alpha Place (now Omega Place), King's Cross, and in 1893 offices were taken at 20 Cheapside in the City of London.

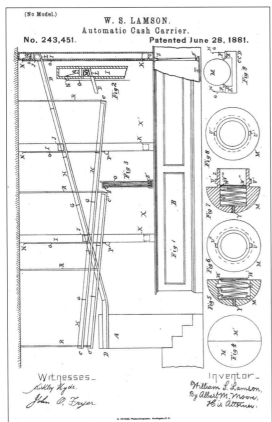

(No Model.)

W. S. LAMSON.
Automatic Cash Carrier.

No. 243,451.   Patented June 28, 1881.

Witnesses_
Kirkley Hyde.
John O. Fryer.

Inventor_
William S. Lamson,
By Albert M. Moore,
His attorney.

A diagram from the earliest patent granted to W. S. Lamson, US patent number 243451, in 1881. It shows the inclined rails and hollow cash balls. It was filed on 14th February 1881 but another patent of his had been filed earlier, on 3rd December 1879.

A cash-ball system at Beamish, the North of England Open Air Museum. The system is displayed in a reconstructed Co-op shop, which is in two parts with the cash office between. The equipment in the drapery department came from the Co-op in Crook, County Durham, and that in the hardware department from the Dean Motorcycle Company, Newcastle upon Tyne.

1. (Above) The cash and 'divvy' ticket are placed in a cash ball.

2. (Right) A close-up of the lift, showing the flaps that hold the ball in place.

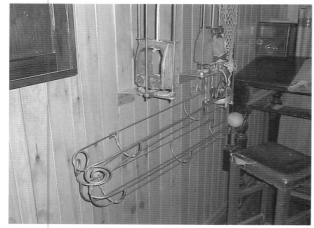

3. The receiving station in the cash office with storage rails and two lifts, for despatching the change.

4. A point on the upper set of rails. When the larger-size ball hits the trigger it is diverted along the curved branch.

5. At the intermediate station in the drapery department, the larger ball operates a trigger and drops down the ramp to the sales point.

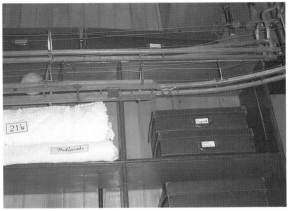

6. A receiving station at the counter. A 'sock' is used to break the fall of the ball. The balls are solid replicas, which are better able to stand up to the constant use.

A cash-ball system at Alexander Moon Ltd, Galway, Ireland, in 1965. There were eight stations.

The cash-ball system

The carrier was a hollow wooden ball, about the size of a croquet ball. It unscrewed into two halves, and the money and receipt were placed inside, held in place by a disc fixed on a spring. The ball was then reassembled and placed in a lift to raise it to the track, which was near the ceiling. To work the lift, the sales assistant pulled a cord that passed over a pulley at the top of the lift. When it reached the track, a flap dropped and the ball rolled out and along the track, which sloped down to the cash office. The assistant could then deal with wrapping the customer's purchase and perhaps interest him or her in buying something else too.

The track consisted of two wooden rails about 3 inches (7.5 cm) apart. Hoops fixed to the rails supported wires that ran alongside the track and stopped the balls from falling off. At the cash office the track ended and the ball fell down, generally through a twisted mesh 'sock' to break its fall, on to a storage rail. This could accommodate several balls until the cashier was able to deal with them.

The cashier picked up the ball, removed the money, noted the transaction and placed the receipt back inside with any change due. In a Co-op shop she would also record the transaction against the member's number for calculating the dividend due. The carrier was reassembled and raised by a lift to the return track, which sloped down from the office to the sales point.

At the sales point the ball again dropped from the track, usually through a 'sock' to slow it down, and on to a leather pad. The assistant removed the ball, took out the receipt and change and counted the change back to the customer. She then placed it back on a shorter storage rail for reuse.

A cash-ball system at Topliss, the drapers, at Louth, Lincolnshire, in about 1975 – then possibly the last cash-ball system operating in Britain. (Above) The system operated over two floors. Here Miss Lorraine Parrish is dropping a ball down a tube to the cashier on the ground floor. (Right) Mrs M. Botting, who had worked at the shop from 1940, places a ball in the hand lift at the downstairs station.

Switches

To avoid having a separate set of tracks to and from each station, which would require a large amount of space at the cash office, points (or 'switches' in American terminology) were used. On the journey to the office no route selection was necessary – all balls finished up at the same place – but on the return journey the balls had to be routed to the correct station. This was achieved by making the balls for each station of a slightly different diameter. At each switch there was a trigger above the track, which would be activated by larger balls but not by smaller ones. The larger ball would be diverted but the smaller one would continue along the track to the next station. After the trigger had been activated it would swing back by gravity. There were two types of switch: one operated on the level and diverted larger balls along the 'branch line' while smaller balls continued straight on. In the other type the larger ball caused a section of track to slope down and discharge the ball from the track, while smaller balls did not trigger the ramp and continued on.

Advantages and disadvantages

The *Modern Draper* commented in 1924 that, although the cash-ball system was not a decorative one, it had no very complicated mechanism and the reason for any breakdown could quickly be observed and attended to. There were no moving parts to wear out apart from the switches and the balls themselves, and no power source was required. However, one danger was that the ball might fall off the track and smash the glass display case below it (wire carriers were less liable to such accidents). Where a large number of stations were being served, a cash office with sufficient space was needed, though the use of points helped to reduce this. A high ceiling was also essential to achieve the required gradient on a long run.

Advertisement for Lamson cable carriers, September 1907.

A cable system in an 'unidentified department store, Brooklyn, 1910'. The book 'New York Interiors at the Turn of the Century' assigns it to the Abraham & Straus department store.

CABLE AND WIRE SYSTEMS

Cable systems

In these systems, the carrier was a small cash box that slid along tracks. It was propelled by a continuous cable, driven by a small steam engine or later by an electric motor. The tracks were rather intrusive but the design looks quite elegant in the photograph of the Brooklyn store. Above the stations the carriage passed over a ramp or else dropped down vertically to the counter. The position of the clamp on the box identified which station it belonged to and caused it to be detached at the correct one.

Joseph C. Martin of Vermont patented a system of this kind in 1882. US patent number 1176807, awarded to George Amsden of Massachusetts in 1916 and assigned to the Lamson Company, shows a design very much like the one at Brooklyn. They seem to have been popular in the USA and are referred to in several memories of locations in North America, but no examples have been found in Britain. Belk's store in Charlotte, North Carolina, had a cable system before it was replaced by pneumatic tubes in 1927. It provided a constant background noise of whirring and clicking as the carriers passed over the ramps. Occasional derailments brought the system to a halt until a sales clerk climbed a ladder and restored it.

At Disneyland Paris the Emporium has a reconstruction of a cable system based on the Brooklyn photograph. It was designed so that it could be left running without intervention by staff.

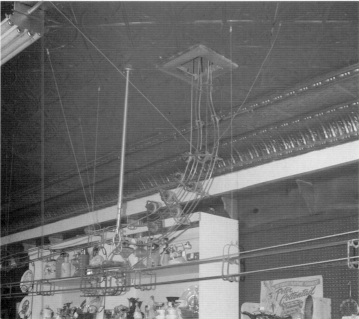

The Lamson cable
system installed in
1915 at the former
Joyner's store at 30
Main Street North,
Moose Jaw,
Saskatchewan,
Canada. It had
over 1000 feet (300
metres) of track
and in 2003 was
claimed to be 'the
world's largest
operational
Lamson Cash
Carrier system'. It
served three levels
of the building and
had fifteen sales
stations. Tragically,
the building burned
down on 1st
January 2004.

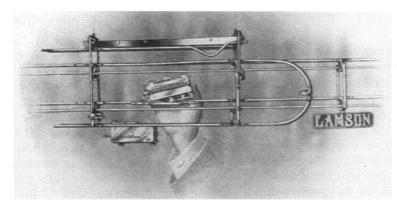

A station on a Lamson automatic cable carrier from 'The Story of a Service Idea' (1912).

Rapid Wire

Wire systems are probably the best-remembered kind of cash conveyor in Britain and the best-represented in museums. The money and receipt were placed in a small wooden cup, which was attached to a brass trolley by a bayonet fitting. Unlike the cable systems, the wire was fixed and the carrier was suspended from pulleys that ran along the wire. A separate wire (or pair of wires in some systems) connected each sales station to the cash office.

Robert McCarty of Detroit, Michigan, took out a series of patents relating to wire carriers in 1884 and 1885. The invention was probably licensed to the Rapid Service Store Railway Company of Detroit. Lamson took control of this company in 1887 and marketed the system under the name Rapid. Wire systems were less intrusive than the cash-ball system, easier to erect and quicker in operation. They needed less space at the cashier's office and so were suitable for smaller shops. Lamson's agent in London had started selling cash-ball systems in 1885 and was offering wire systems from about 1894. Systems could be leased or bought outright. Kerr's of Dartford, Kent, rented theirs from the

A close-up of the handle and trigger of a Rapid Wire propulsion now at the Age Exchange Reminiscence Centre, Blackheath, London SE3.

13

1. A carriage being despatched from a Rapid Wire propulsion.

A wire system at Anscombe's of Harpenden, Hertfordshire, in October 1973. This was one of the late-surviving wire systems in Britain. It had five lines of Rapid Wire design and one Gipe, used for the line that went upstairs. It closed on 21st August 1982.

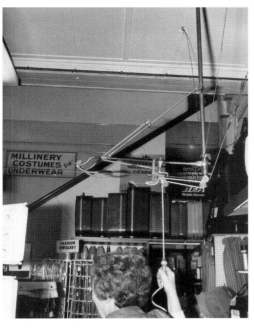

2. (Above left) Another view of a propulsion.

3. (Above right) The cash office. The Gipe line is distinguished by having a horizontal handle attached to a lever, whereas the Rapid Wire lines have handles hanging from cords.

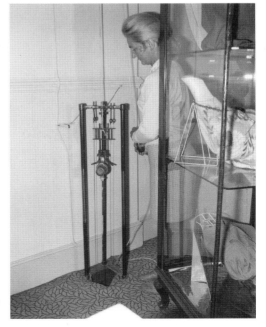

4. The 'uplift' used to carry the carrier up to the first floor.

Mr Bernard Williams, the last owner of Kerr's Drapers in Dartford, Kent, operating the Lamson Rapid Wire propulsion. The shop closed in 1979 and part of the system is now in Dartford Museum. (Kentish Times Newspapers)

Lamson Company from 1900 to 1970, when they purchased it for half a crown (12.5 pence).

The Rapid Wire system used a single cable, from which the carriage hung by two pulleys. It was propelled by means of a catapult device (technically called a 'propulsion') at each end. This was in the form of a right-angled triangle. The vertical pole was attached to the ceiling, a horizontal rod ran parallel to the wire, and a strut at about 45 degrees to each supported the rod. There was a slider hanging from the rod with a catch that engaged the carriage and a pulley. A cord passed round this pulley, round another pulley attached to the bottom of the vertical pole, and was secured to the slider.

To propel the carriage, the operator pulled the handle at the other end of the cord. This pulled the slider and carriage back along the rod towards the pole, tightening the elastic that was fixed to the slider and the middle of the diagonal strut. At a certain point (adjusted for the distance of the journey) the slider contacted a trigger, which released the catch and launched the carriage on its way. When it reached its destination it engaged the catch in the propulsion there.

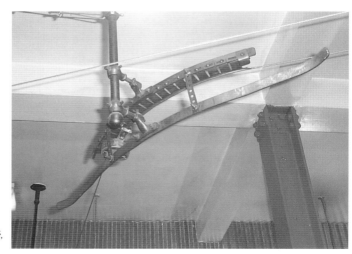

A curve in the system taken from Clery's department store but now at the Bad Ass Café, Dublin.

Right: *A drawing of an Air-Line propulsion and carriage from a Lamson brochure. There are two wires – the carrier is suspended from the bottom one and the top one is used to provide extra rigidity. The propelling cord loops around the back of the carriage. Because there is no elastic, no diagonal strut is needed.*

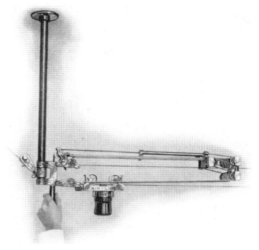

Below: *The two-wire system illustrated in a patent granted to S. W. Barr in 1887 (US patent number 358717). This was the precursor of the Gipe design.*

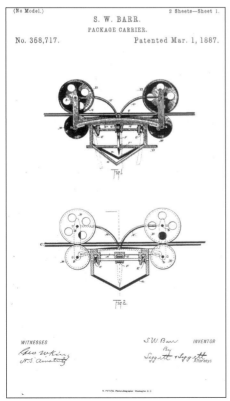

Carriages could travel round corners and even between floors. The 'curve car' had a shorter wheelbase and cut-away sides.

Rapid Wire systems were still being publicised in 1962. Some of the last customers in Europe were bingo halls and Amsterdam's Schiphol Airport (for carrying air tickets). In a letter of 1974 Mr Tribe of the Lamson Company reported that there were about fifty Rapid Wire systems remaining in Britain.

Air-Line

Various other methods of propulsion were devised, no doubt to get round Lamson's patents. Emanuel Gipe of Chicago, Illinois, patented an arrangement with a cord looped round three sets of pulleys. A sharp tug on the handle would give the carriage sufficient impetus to travel up to 200 feet (60 metres) on the level. This design was used by the Air-Line Company, based in the USA. Lamson took them over and the carriages typically have 'Air-Line' on one side and 'Lamson' on the other. This system had supplanted the Rapid in the USA by the 1920s. It is still in place at the Yellowstone

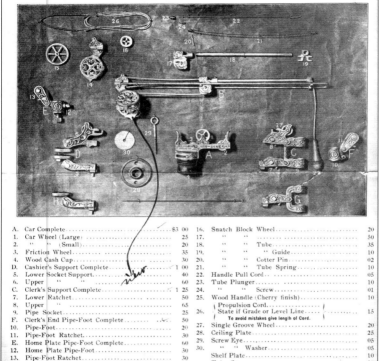

==PRICE LIST==

AIR LINE CASH CARRIERS.

A.	Car Complete	$3 00	16.	Snatch Block Wheel	20
1.	Car Wheel (Large)	25	17.	" "	50
2.	" " (Small)	20	18.	" " Tube	35
3.	Friction Wheel	35	19.	" " " Guide	10
4.	Wood Cash Cup	30	20.	" " " Cotter Pin	02
D.	Cashier's Support Complete	1 00	21.	" " " Tube Spring	10
5.	Lower Socket Support	40	22.	Handle Pull Cord	05
6.	Upper " "	60	23.	Tube Plunger	10
C.	Clerk's Support Complete	1 25	24.	" " Screw	01
7.	Lower Ratchet	50	25.	Wood Handle (Cherry finish)	10
8.	Upper "	65	26.	Propulsion Cord. / State if Grade or Level Line / To avoid mistakes give length of Cord.	15
9.	Pipe Socket	25			
F.	Clerk's End Pipe-Foot Complete	50	27.	Single Groove Wheel	20
10.	Pipe-Foot	20	28.	Ceiling Plate	25
11.	Pipe-Foot Ratchet	30	29.	Screw Eye	05
E.	Home Plate Pipe-Foot Complete	60	30.	" " Washer	05
12.	Home Plate Pipe-Foot	30		Shelf Plate	10
13.	Pipe-Foot Ratchet	30		Tube Stop	30
B.	Propulsion Complete	3 50		Track Wire (Special) 10c lb., 66 ft. to lb.	
14.	Pulley Support	1 75		Brace " (")10c " 34 " "	
15.	" " Wheel	35			

A price list for Air-Line carriers from about 1916. A 'complete car' cost $3; now they sell at auction for up to $250.

Mercantile Store in Sidney, Montana, and the former Lown's department store at Penn Yan, New York State (featured on the Lemelson Center's videos). Although it was advertised in Britain, no British examples have been found.

Gipe

A system involving a carriage with two sets of wheels was invented by Samuel Barr of Mansfield, Ohio. The upper set ran on top of one wire and the lower set ran below a second wire. At the sending station the wires were pulled apart by a lever arrangement, and this propelled the carriage to the destination station, where the lever was positioned so that the wires were close together. One shop known to have had a Barr system in 1900 is The Grand Leader store of McLeansboro, Illinois. In December 1889 the stock of the Barr Cash & Package Carrier Company was sold to the Lamson Consolidated Store Service Company.

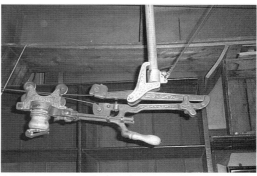

*A Gipe system propulsion and carrier at Grout's. Note that
the carrier has four wheels and runs on two wires. The
handle is attached to the lower lever and is almost
horizontal.*

*The lines converging at the cash office at
Grout's. The Gipe cash-carrier system
connected four sales points at the front of
the shop and three at the rear with the
cashier's office in the middle.*

In 1908 Gipe set up a company in London to market an improved version of the Barr
carrier. Instead of a single straight lever to which the wires were fixed, this design had two
levers pivoted at one end, with a wire attached to each at the other end. A handle on the
lower lever allowed them to be pulled apart, thus pulling the wires apart too. As soon as
the carriage had been sent on its way the levers could be closed again, and the wires
remained close together. This made for a neater appearance and reduced the amount of
headroom needed for the original version. Gipe propulsions can easily be recognised by
the near-horizontal handle, as compared to the vertical handle on the end of the cord in
the Rapid Wire system.

Before Gipe returned to Canada in 1909 he sold an interest in his Gipe Carrier Company
Ltd to Lamson. The system proved quite popular and was sold until the 1940s. In 1944 it
was renamed the Lamson Ariel system.

Dart Cash Carrier Company

Other companies also entered the wire-carrier market in Britain. The Dart Cash Carrier
Company was established by William Edwards, a grocer from Stoke-on-Trent, to market
a gravity carrier that he had patented in 1918. He introduced a number of other designs,

A Dart cash system at Bromsgrove Museum, Worcestershire. (Above) The propulsion and carrier. The equipment came from the firm of Harry Cooper of Willenhall, Staffordshire, which closed around 1988. (Right) The propulsion at the cash office in the museum display.

including one using a spring to propel the carriage. Lamson bought a 51 per cent stake in the firm in 1927 and became sole owner in 1948. Systems were installed until 1958. The firm was based in Stoke-on-Trent and Lamson moved to a new factory there in 1974.

A cash-basket system. Cash baskets could carry purchases as well as the payment. The basket had a place on which to attach a small leather cup for the money and sales slip. While one assistant dealt with the payment another would wrap the goods, and the basket would be returned with the parcel and change. The basket was raised by means of a cord up to the carriage and it then attached itself to the carriage. No British examples of cash baskets are known.

PNEUMATIC TUBE SYSTEMS

In pneumatic tube systems the carrier is a hollow cylinder about 5 or 6 inches long (12–15 cm), sealed at each end but with an opening in the side. It is opened or closed by twisting one end relative to the other. The carriers are numbered to identify which station they belong to, and the tubes are similarly numbered in the cash office. The ends are covered in felt to provide an air seal in the tube and perhaps to soften the impact as the carrier travels round bends or reaches its destination.

Two tubes are required between each station and the central cash office – one for each direction. In the traditional Lamson systems they are $2\frac{1}{4}$ inches in diameter (5.7 cm). The carrier is propelled along the tube by a difference in air pressure in front of and behind it: the space in front is a partial vacuum maintained by an air pump or turbine, while the space behind is at atmospheric pressure. No special equipment is needed to travel between floors and the tubes can be concealed beneath flooring or behind walls.

An advertisement by Lamson claimed 'communication to and from cashier or counting house in six seconds'. With a belt system in the cash office, the carrier could be returned before the sales assistant had finished wrapping the goods.

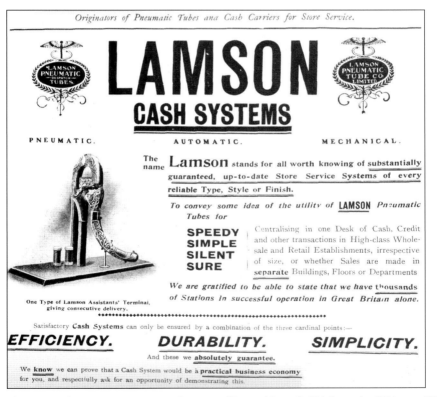

An advertisement for a Lamson pneumatic tube system. ('Drapers' Record', 17th September 1904, page 787)

History

The pneumatic tube was introduced into department stores in 1880 by John Wanamaker, the Philadelphia retail magnate. He had previously installed such a system in the US Post Office while he was Postmaster General. A contemporary article describes there being two tubes to each counter – one for each direction. Each carrier was exactly the diameter of a silver dollar (smaller than the later Lamson systems) and could hold thirty such coins. 'By means of steam engine and exhaust pump in the cellar, with proper attachments leading therefrom, the air is being constantly exhausted at the cashier's end of the tube and the counter end of the tube of each pair.'

A number of firms were active in selling pneumatic tube systems to shops in the 1890s. The Bostedo Company, which had been in existence since at least 1888, opened an agency in London in 1897. The Lamson Company bought out Bostedo and established the Lamson Pneumatic Tube Company Ltd in May 1899 with a factory at Albion Street near King's Cross.

By March 1900 four drapery stores in London had pneumatic tube systems: Robinson & Cleaver in Regent Street, Bon Marché in Brixton, J. R. Roberts in Stratford and the newly opened John Barnes & Company in Finchley Road. However, it

> A Lamson pneumatic tube terminal at Cumberland Toy and Model Museum. It came from Brown's (later Mark Taylor's) of Workington, Cumbria, and is on loan to the museum.

A general view of the terminal.

The inlet for inserting the carriers.

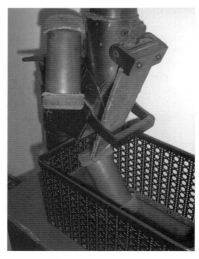

The outlet where the carriers dropped through the hinged door into the basket.

A Rebesi hand-operated terminal from the British Cash and Parcel Conveyers Ltd. ('Draper and Drapery Times', 18th July 1931, page iii)

was to be some years before pneumatic tubes became profitable. In 1911 the Lamson directors closed both the store service and pneumatic tube factories at King's Cross and moved all manufacturing to a new site at Hythe Road, Willesden Junction. In January 1937 the Lamson Engineering Company Ltd was incorporated to acquire the business and trading assets of Lamson Store Service Company Ltd and Lamson Pneumatic Tube Company Ltd, and Lamson Engineering remained prosperous up to the 1960s. Manufacturing was moved to a new factory in Stoke-on-Trent in 1974, just as British industry entered a period of recession.

In 1976 Lamson Engineering was taken over by a rival company, Dialled Despatches Ltd of Gosport in Hampshire. They manufactured a pneumatic tube system, not intended for use in shops, in which the carrier could be directed to a particular terminal by setting a dial that controlled electrical contacts. The firm became DD Lamson Ltd. It has been the subject of further takeovers and is in 2004 incorporated with BVC (a descendant of the British Vacuum Cleaner Company) as part of Barloworld Ltd.

Other manufacturers in Britain were Sturtevant Engineering Company of London and the Dart Cash Carrier Company Ltd. Co-op shops often chose Dart systems because J. F. Edwards, Dart's managing director, had strong links with the Co-operative movement.

Stations

The early terminals were often very ornate, as in the Lamson advertisement of 1904. Later ones were of similar shape but less ornate, with a vertical tube bent downwards to slow down the carrier and allow it to drop into a basket.

The Pneu-Art design was developed by Lamson for the new system installed in Harrods in Knightsbridge, London, in 1935. The two tubes were enclosed in a metal box with a hinged glass door. They were finished to harmonise with different departments: silver in the gown department, bronze in the men's outfitting department, and so on. The terminals could be recessed into the wall or stanchions and so they were quite well concealed.

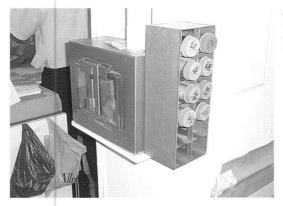

A 'Pneu-Art' terminal, station 28, in the kitchenware department at Arding & Hobbs with adjacent pigeon-holes for carriers.

Station 21 by the ladies' knitwear section at Arding & Hobbs, with carriers of two different lengths.

Here, exposed tubes make a right-angled bend in the basement at Arding & Hobbs, where appearance was perhaps not so important.

A later pneumatic tube system at Arding & Hobbs, Clapham Junction, London SW11, in February 2003.

Cash desks

For systems of moderate size a gravity desk in the cash office allowed the carriers to drop down a chute to the cashier. Larger systems used a belt desk, where the containers dropped on to a conveyor belt and were carried to a row of cashiers. After being dealt with, they were again conveyed by belt to a despatcher for return to the department, or they were despatched by the cashier herself. At Simpsons in London the belt travelled at about 400 feet (120 metres) per minute. The cash desk installed at Harrods in 1935 had forty-eight cashiers' positions.

Separators could be fitted for routing the cash and credit carriers separately. The cash carriers would be directed to the cashier in the cash office, while the credit carriers would be conveyed to authorisers, perhaps in a different room. They were distinguished by various means – different colours, or smooth carriers for cash and corrugated carriers for credit. Some allowed automatic separation, either by means of a small hole in the end which engaged a 'tripper' that threw the carrier on to the upper belt, or by one type being made of steel that could be picked up by a magnetic device.

Turbines

The vacuum plant or 'blower' was usually in the basement. In the early days it might be powered by a steam engine but later on electric motors were used. The blower contained

The central cash desk installed by Sturtevant Engineering Company Ltd for John Banner Ltd of Sheffield. This kind of cash desk was used in larger stores – this one served seventy-five stations. Sturtevant was another offshoot of an American company and competed with Lamson during the 1930s and 1940s. In about 1948 they sold their pneumatic tube interests to Lamson Engineering.

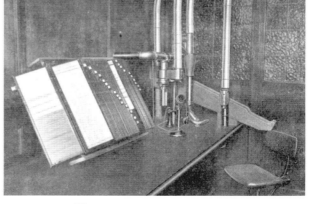

A credit-sanctioning desk. On the left is a 'visible index' for checking account details; the Sturtevant pneumatic tube equipment is on the right. (Both pictures from 'Store Interior Planning & Display' by Edward A. Hammond, Blandford, 1939.)

A pneumatic tube system at Jacksons of Reading in 2003. The system is still used for making change at the cash office. (Above left) The Lamson Gravity Cash Desk in the cash office. (Above right) The blower in the basement, powered by the electric motor in front. Air is blown out by the turbine through the tube on the right, which produces a partial vacuum in the tube on the left. This tube leads up to the cash office on the ground floor. The plate at the bottom of this tube permits loose papers such as notes that have fallen out of carriers to be removed. (Below) A station on the ground floor.

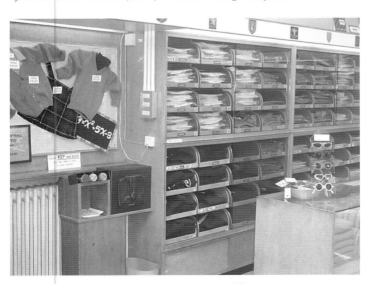

A plastic carrier or 'pod' from a modern DD Lamson system.

A carrier being inserted into a DD Lamson terminal at the Wilkinson supermarket in Burgess Hill, West Sussex. There is one terminal for each checkout and the terminal incorporates an intercom system.

a fan, which took the form of a large disc with a number of vanes radiating from its centre. This was enclosed in a casing with an inlet pipe at the centre and an outlet (or exhaust) pipe on the circumference. When the rotor revolved, the air was flung outwards by centrifugal force into the exhaust pipe. Air was drawn in to replace it, so causing a vacuum in the inlet pipe, which was used to draw the carriers through the transmission tubes. In the earlier systems the turbine drew air through all the tubes, whether or not a carrier was travelling. Later systems reduced the cost of operation by means of controls that closed off the tube from the turbine when not needed. The system at Blake's in Maidstone used a foot pump that became less efficient as it got older, requiring some strength to send carriers up to the fashion department on the first floor.

The turbine plant could also be used for operating vacuum-cleaning equipment and tubes for carrying paperwork such as despatch notes.

Modern systems

Pneumatic tubes have made a comeback in supermarkets. They are sometimes used at checkouts to carry cash to a more secure central office and reduce the amount held in the tills, which are usually close to the exit. They avoid the need for someone to carry the money through the store. A single tube serves each till, of larger diameter than the usual $2^1/4$ inches (5.7 cm), and the empty containers are returned by hand. The tubes and carriers are made of plastic with rubber seals.

Other applications

Pneumatic tube conveyors were in use elsewhere well before their use in shops. The first practical application was in 1853 between the central offices of the Electric & International Telegraph Company on Telegraph Street in London and the Stock Exchange. Tubes and other systems for carrying messages on paper were common in bunkers and war rooms, and hotels offered every modern convenience 'including pneumatic tube-messaging'. Large libraries used them to carry request slips to the different areas of the book stack. They are still being installed in hospitals to carry medical samples to laboratories.

Advertisement for the Bostedo Package and Cash Carrier Company, showing basket and pneumatic tube apparatus. Date unknown.

CASH CARRIERS IN MEMORY, LITERATURE AND FILM

Many memories of working with cash carriers have been recorded. At Blyth & Fargo's store in Evanston, Wyoming, 'if the incorrect change was made, they [the clerks] would rattle the wire and send the cup back down'. In Ireland Mr Shaw of Shaw's department stores described how the sales staff had to keep a record of each sale, and at various times of the day, but particularly the end, they would have to agree their totals with the office total. All sales staff used to have a pencil behind their ear with which they would tap the wire if the office delayed in sending back change, to tell them to hurry up. Sometimes the sales staff sent several sales at once to try to confuse the office staff over the change they had to return. Not to be outdone, the office staff would then send back all the change in one go, and unless the sales staff remembered what to expect they had problems.

Taunting the office staff seems to have been a favourite pastime. A former employee of the Lewes Co-op wrote: 'There were about five railways which went along to the cash

A cartoon from the 'Daily Chronicle', 18th July 1924.

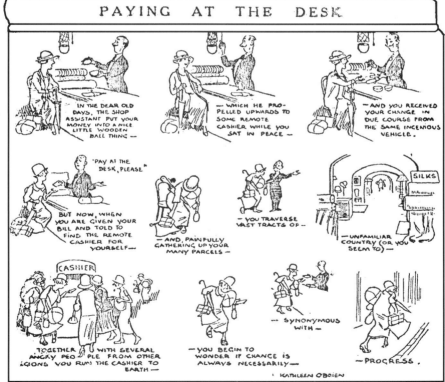

desk – the girl used to put the change in and send it back. Occasionally if things were slack we used to sort of wind up the girls in the office by either putting in false messages or a dead mouse … much to the consternation of the shop manager!' Another account of causing uproar in the office by despatching a mouse is given in a history of Arnotts of Dublin. The passengers in Australia were more exotic: a spider or a lizard was 'not uncommon' at the River Don Trading Company.

In New York State Jim Kerbull, the former owner of Lown's store in Penn Yan, recounts that dogs used to race the Air-Line carrier back and forth (though they were not supposed to be in the store). Mr Hughes of T. P. Hughes of Tenby in Pembrokeshire also mentioned dogs chasing and barking at his system, which as it was a pneumatic tube is perhaps more surprising.

A number of novels that include scenes in shops contain references to cash carriers. H. G. Wells was apprenticed to a draper and the shop appears as Edwin Shalford's Drapery Bazaar at Folkestone in *Kipps* (1905). Shalford points to the 'overhead change carrier' and enters into calculations on how many minutes are saved by it in a year. In Frances Donovan's novel *The Saleslady* (1929) the new assistant at McElroys lives in dread of having her carrier returned with a red rubber band round it. This would mean that she had made a mistake and would have to take it to her section manager. Anyone discovering a mistake received a 'premium'.

Mr Mog Edwards in Dylan Thomas's *Under Milk Wood* (1954) declares, 'I am a draper mad with love … I have come to take you away to my Emporium on the hill, where the change hums on wires.'

The play *Madame Louise: A Farce in Three Acts* by Vernon Sylvaine (1946) is set in the Madame Louise Gown Shop, well off Bond Street. The stage directions specify 'an old-fashioned cash-change arrangement – with not more than ten feet of runway'. Mr Mould boasts: 'We're one of the few London houses still retaining a cash expediter.' Until the 1970s Lamson kept a Rapid Wire set specially boxed up to lend to societies putting on this play.

In the Ealing Studios film *Kind Hearts and Coronets* (1949), Louis Mazzini, played by Dennis Price, is forced by family circumstances to take a job in a draper's shop, in which he is seen using a wire system. He then moves up to a larger establishment fitted with pneumatic tubes. A pneumatic tube system also features in *The Longest Night* (1936), produced by Lucien Hubbard and Samuel Marx. *The Magic Box*, a film directed by John Boulting for the Festival of Britain (1951), stars Robert Donat as William Friese-Greene, whose second wife works in the glove department of a store where there is a Lamson Rapid Wire system.

A stirring account of the opening of a cash railway is given by the *Middlesbrough Daily Exchange*, 3rd March 1887:

At 10.30 this (Saturday) morning the Mayor of Middlesbrough (Mr Amos Hinton) opened the Cash Railway at Messrs John Hedley & Co.'s noted drapery establishment, Linthorpe-road, Middlesbrough. The mayor's daughter was the first purchaser, and the money and check were despatched to the cash desk, and returned with the change in a very short time, and was handed to Miss Hinton amid loud cheers from the large company assembled. The Mayor said, Messrs Hedley and Co. have this morning introduced to the Middlesbrough public one of the most ingenious contrivances that it had been his pleasure to witness, and which was called a Cash Railway. The cash received from the customer was put into one of the balls, which was then closed up and sent along the rails to the cashier...

He then said that having sent the money ball rolling, he hoped it would roll merrily all through the year, not only in that establishment, but in every tradesman's in Middlesbrough and throughout the country. (Loud cheers.)

FURTHER READING

'All Change for the Overhead Cash Railway'. *This England*, Spring 1975, pages 32–3. Includes a letter from Mrs Proctor.

Hammond, A. Edward. *Store Interior Planning & Display*. Blandford, 1939. Chapter 6 is on service equipment.

Liffen, John. 'The Development of Cash Handling Systems for Shops and Department Stores'. *Transactions of the Newcomen Society*, 71, no. 1 (1999–2000), pages 79–101.

Lovett, Vivien. *Kennards of Croydon: The Store that Entertained to Sell*. Self-published, 2000. Contains two photographs of the cash room.

The Modern Draper: The Draper's Encyclopaedia. Caxton, 1924. Volume 2 includes two plates showing cash carriers and Volume 3 includes a discussion on the handling of cash.

Proctor, Molly G. *Are You Being Served, Madam? Shopping at the Drapers in Bygone Kent*. Meresborough Books, 1987.

See also the author's Cash Railway Website: www.cashrailway.co.uk

Advertisement for the Air-Line Carrier Company, 1901.

PLACES TO VISIT

GREAT BRITAIN AND IRELAND

Age Exchange Reminiscence Centre, 11 Blackheath Village, London SE3 9LA. Telephone: 020 8318 9105. Website: www.age-exchange.org.uk (Rapid Wire system.)

Bad Ass Café, 9–11 Crown Alley, Temple Bar, Dublin 2, Ireland. Telephone: (+353) 1 671 2596. Website: www.badasscafe.com (Rapid Wire system taken from Clery's department store; in working order.)

Beamish: North of England Open Air Museum, Beamish, Stanley, County Durham DH9 0RG. Telephone: 0191 370 4000. Website: www.beamish.org.uk (Extensive cash-ball system in operation.)

Bromsgrove Museum, 26 Birmingham Road, Bromsgrove, Worcestershire B61 0DD. Telephone: 01527 831809. Website: www.bromsgrove.gov.uk (Dart Cash system.)

Crich Tramway Village, Crich, Matlock, Derbyshire DE4 5DP. Telephone: 0870 7587267. Website: www.tramway.co.uk (Lamson Ariel system.)

Cumberland Toy and Model Museum, Banks Court, Market Place, Cockermouth, Cumbria CA13 9NG. Telephone: 01900 827606. Website: www.toymuseum.co.uk (Pneumatic tube station.)

Dartford Borough Museum, Market Street, Dartford, Kent DA1 1EU. Telephone: 01322 224739. Website: www.dartford.gov.uk/community/museum/ (Rapid Wire system from Kerr's of Dartford; in working order.)

Fleur de Lis Heritage Museum, 10–13 Preston Street, Faversham, Kent ME13 8NS. Telephone: 01795 534542. Website: www.faversham.org/society/museum.asp (Display on Rapid Wire system with a few parts from Child's shop.)

Jacksons, Jackson's Corner, 1–9 Kings Road, Reading RG1 3AS. Telephone: 0118 957 4477. Website: www.jacksonsofreading.co.uk (Lamson pneumatic tube system; in use.)

Museum of London, London Wall, London EC2Y 5HN. Telephone: 020 7600 3699. Website: www.museumoflondon.org.uk (Rapid Wire system.)

Trowbridge Museum, The Shires Shopping Centre, Court Street, Trowbridge, Wiltshire BA14 8AT. Telephone: 01225 751339. Website: www.trowbridgemuseum.co.uk (Gipe system.)

AUSTRALIA

Up-to-Date Store, Coolamon, NSW 2701. Telephone: (+61) 2 69272 492. Website: coolamon.local-e.nsw.gov.au/about (Claimed to be the only cash-ball system still *in situ.*)

UNITED STATES OF AMERICA

Antiques Emporium, 223 Main Street, Smithfield, Virginia 23430. Telephone: (+1 757) 357 3304. Website: www.pearllinepress.com/emporium/html/antiques_emporium.htm (Air-Line system.)

Lown's House of Shoppes, 131 Main Street, Penn Yan, New York 14527. Telephone: (+1 315) 531 8343. Website: www.lownsshoppes.com (Lamson Air-Line system.)